WORLD OF WONDER · WOW

THE AWESOME BOOK OF

PREHISTORIC ANIMALS

Get ready to hear your kids say, "Wow! That's awesome!" as they dive into this fun, informative, question-answering series of books! Students—and teachers and parents—will learn things about the world around them that they never knew before!

This approach to education seeks to promote an interest in learning by answering questions kids have always wondered about. When books answer questions that kids already want to know the answers to, kids love to read those books, fostering a love for reading and learning, the true keys to lifelong education.

Colorful graphics are labeled and explained to connect with visual learners, while in-depth explanations of each subject will connect with those who prefer reading or listening as their learning style.

This educational series makes learning fun through many levels of interaction. The in-depth information combined with fantastic illustrations promote learning and retention, while question and answer boxes reinforce the subject matter to promote higher order thinking.

Teachers and parents love this series because it engages young people, sparking an interest and desire in learning. It doesn't feel like work to learn about a new subject with books this interactive and interesting.

This set of books will be an addition to your home or classroom library that everyone will enjoy. And, before you know it, you, too, will be saying, "Wow! That's awesome!"

"People cannot learn by having information pressed into their brains. Knowledge has to be sucked into the brain, not pushed in. First, one must create a state of mind that craves knowledge, interest, and wonder. You can teach only by creating an urge to know." - Victor Weisskopf

© 2012 Flowerpot Press

Contents under license from Aladdin Books Ltd.

Flowerpot Press
142 2nd Avenue North
Franklin, TN 37064

Flowerpot Press is a division of Kamalu, LLC, Franklin, TN, U.S.A., and Mitso Media, Inc., Oakville, ON, Canada.

ISBN 978-1-77093-780-2

Illustrators:
Dave Burroughs
James Field (SGA)
Darren Harvey
Alex Pang
Francis Phillipps
Mike Saunders
Ian Thompson
Ross Watton (SGA)
Cartoons: Jo Moore

American Edition Editor:
Johannah Gilman Paiva

Designer: Flick, Book Design & Graphics

American Redesign:
Jonas Fearon Bell

Printed in China.

CONTENTS

INTRODUCTION

During the history of Earth, there have been far more extinct animals than there are living ones today. In fact, life was almost wiped out before it had a chance to get going. When life began many millions of years ago, there was little oxygen in the atmosphere. All early plant-like life forms relied on other gases to breathe. But as they grew, they produced oxygen, which had the effect of poisoning them. This was the first mass extinction on the planet. Then, some survivors began to use oxygen as animals do today. Over time, many different species evolved to occupy every place on the planet.

Q: Why watch out for these boxes?

A: They give answers to the questions you always wanted to ask about prehistoric animals.

Zoom in on...

Bits and Pieces

Look out for these boxes to take a closer look at prehistoric animal features.

Awesome Facts

Watch out for these diamonds to learn more about the truly weird and wonderful facts about prehistoric animals and their world.

ENDANGERED AND EXTINCT

As life evolved, primitive animal species were gradually replaced by more refined versions, like the species we see today. The ancient species became extinct—they disappeared forever. Now, many modern species are also threatened with extinction. Sharks, for example, have a 400-million-year-old history, yet several species are now endangered.

SYMBOL DEFINITIONS

In this book, the red X symbol shows an animal that is already extinct. The yellow exclamation point shows an animal whose ancestors have been around since prehistoric times, but is now endangered. (This means that there are a few animals of that species left in the wild.) The green check shows an animal that has survived from prehistoric times. Many of these ancient animals have only recently been rediscovered, but most are still endangered species.

Mammoth

Great white shark

Coelacanth

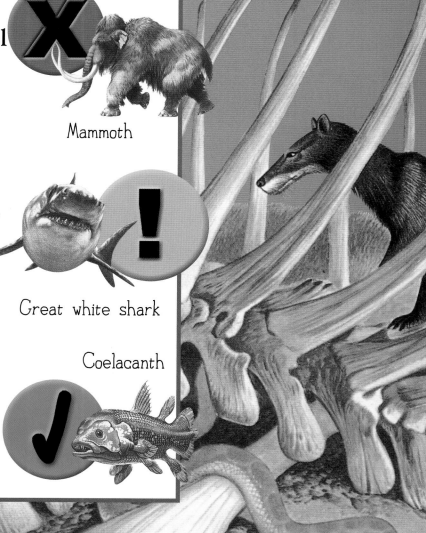

Q: Why do animals become extinct today?

A: Various reasons: destruction of their habitat, removal of their food, overhunting, pollution, or general disturbance that prevents them from breeding. Disturbance can be in the form of "alien" animals, like rats or cats, which are introduced to previously isolated places, such as islands. The aliens compete with or kill the defenseless residents.

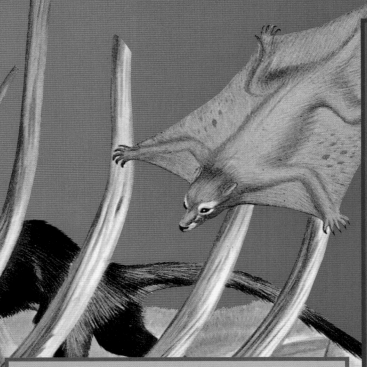

If overcrowded, animals might cross the sea or a mountain range to see if conditions are better on the other side. If they are, the animals will thrive and may develop skills that the original population lacks. In this way, they may become a new species. The new arrivals will compete with local residents and, if they are better equipped, they will often survive while the residents die out.

There were times in prehistory when entire families of species were wiped out as the result of a great catastrophe. It is thought that a meteorite hitting the Earth from space was responsible for the dinosaurs dying out. A species confined to a small area can be wiped out completely just by a flash flood, forest fire, or violent storm. This happened recently in South America: several captive-bred golden lion tamarins (endangered) were released into a forest. There later was a terrible fire there, which almost killed them all.

WHAT IS PREHISTORY?

Prehistory is the time before history—before people began to keep written records of events that influenced their lives. It was also before people affected the state of the planet, when evolution and extinction were purely natural events. We know about prehistory through fossils, the remains of ancient life buried in layers of rock.

Warm period

Ice age

200 million years ago

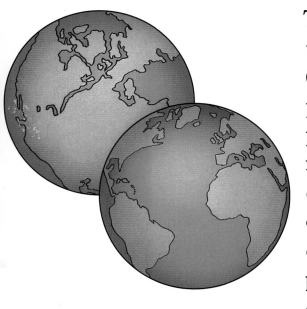

Present day

The ancient Earth was very different from the planet today. The climate and geology (rock formation) have changed often during prehistory, and it is still changing. Weather patterns have shifted, the continents have moved and collided, mountains have risen and been eroded (worn down), and periods of increasing or decreasing ice cover have caused huge variation in sea levels. All these physical events have affected life on Earth, causing some species to die out, but also helping others to survive.

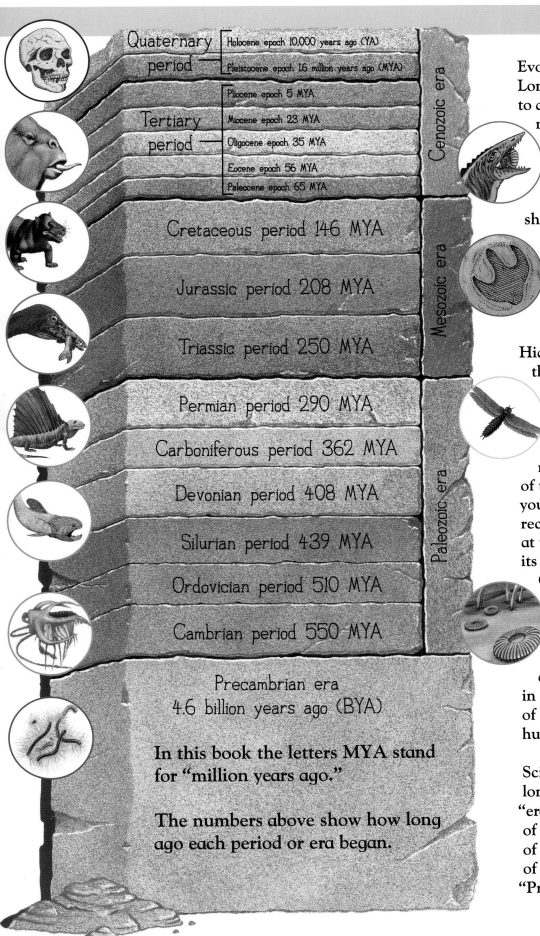

Quaternary period

Holocene epoch 10,000 years ago (YA)	
Pleistocene epoch 1.6 million years ago (MYA)	

Tertiary period

Pliocene epoch 5 MYA
Miocene epoch 23 MYA
Oligocene epoch 35 MYA
Eocene epoch 56 MYA
Paleocene epoch 65 MYA

Cenozoic era

Cretaceous period 146 MYA

Jurassic period 208 MYA

Triassic period 250 MYA

Mesozoic era

Permian period 290 MYA

Carboniferous period 362 MYA

Devonian period 408 MYA

Silurian period 439 MYA

Ordovician period 510 MYA

Cambrian period 550 MYA

Paleozoic era

Precambrian era
4.6 billion years ago (BYA)

In this book the letters MYA stand for "million years ago."

The numbers above show how long ago each period or era began.

Evolution happens in bursts. Long periods of stability lead to animals growing bigger and more specialized. When conditions change, these "specialists" are unable to adapt. The long, stable periods are punctuated by short, sharp shocks that kill off hundreds of species. This enables more adaptable "generalist" species to emerge, develop, and be successful.

Hidden in the rocks are fossils, the stony evidence of what lived in prehistoric times. The rocks in which fossils are found are like a layer of cake, with each layer representing a different period of time. The upper layers are the youngest and contain the most recent fossils. The oldest are at the bottom. Each period had its own dominant animals. The Cambrian period was when all the groups of animals we see today first evolved. The Devonian was the age of fish, and the Jurassic the age of reptiles. We are now in the Holocene epoch (section) of the Quaternary period, and humans dominate the planet.

Scientists group the periods into longer stretches of time called "eras." Each era covers hundreds of millions, sometimes billions, of years. The first 4 billion years of Earth's history is called the "Precambrian era."

EARLY EXPERIMENTS

About 510 MYA, there was an evolutionary "tryout" period, when all the main groups of animals we see today first appeared. Some of these early arrivals survived and evolved into new species. Others were an evolutionary "dead end" and became extinct. Their fossil remains have been found in the ancient rocks of the Burgess Shale in Canada.

Zoom in on...

Hallucigenia

This segmented creature looked like a type of worm that walked on two rows of tentacle-like feet. It had spikes along its back, which it used to defend itself. Its actual shape and number of spikes are still being researched.

Marrella was the first Burgess Shale animal to be found. It is nicknamed the "lace crab" because of its delicate legs and gills.

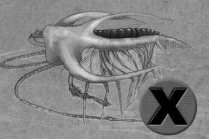

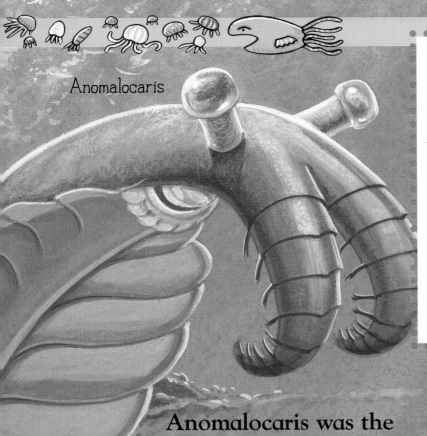
Anomalocaris

Q: How did the Burgess Shale animals die?

A: The animals were trapped by underwater mudflows that swept them off their shallow reefs and into deep water, where they were buried. They are perfectly preserved—including all the soft parts—because they were not exposed to oxygen or bacteria.

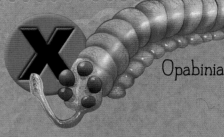
Opabinia

Anomalocaris was the terror of the Cambrian seas. It was a predator, with a hard outer shell, a backbone, and a circular mouth on its underside. Two grasping arms caught its prey. It was about 6.5 feet (2 meters) long, making it the largest animal of its time.

Opabinia was a five-eyed, segmented animal that crawled on the sea bottom. It had a fluid-filled arm on the front of its head, like a vacuum cleaner. It ate bits and pieces that it found in the mud.

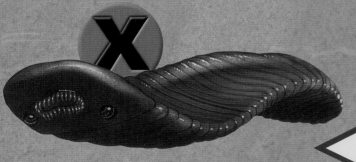
Odontogriphus was about 2.5 inches (6 centimeters) long, and had tiny tentacles and tooth-like structures at its front end.

Awesome Facts
Anomalocaris was first thought to be three animals. It had mouthparts like a jellyfish, a body like a sponge, and arms like a shrimp.

PRIMITIVE SEA CREATURES

Some of the early sea creatures were protected by shells or hard bodies, like shellfish and sea urchins have today. These animals survived for many millions of years, but were gradually knocked out by mass extinction events (see page 18).

Cystoids

Belemnite

Zoom in on...

X

Living fossils

Animals alive today that closely resemble those that lived many millions of years ago are known as "living fossils." One living fossil is the pearly nautilus (below), which looks like an ammonite. These animals have been in the evolutionary slow lane, changing gradually over time.

Belemnites were squid-like predators, with a soft body surrounding a bullet-shaped shell. They had tentacles at one end, but they were armed with hooks rather than suckers. They died out with the dinosaurs about 65 MYA.

Trilobites were hard-shelled, segmented creatures that were shaped like modern wood lice or horseshoe crabs. They first appeared about 540 MYA, and developed into the most diverse (varied) group of animals. There were trilobite meat eaters and plant eaters. They became extinct 300 million years later.

Trilobite

Ammonite fossil

Ammonites were related to octopi and squid. They had a spiral shell divided into sections called "buoyancy chambers," which enabled the ammonite to float. Ammonites disappeared 65 MYA.

Ammonite

Cystoids were globular echinoderms (spiny-bodied animals) on stalks. They were attached to the seabed and lived in small colonies in shallow water. They disappeared about 250 MYA.

Cystoid

Brachiopods are clam-like animals. They were once abundant, but about 250 MYA, 12,000 species were wiped out. Today, just 325 species survive in the deep sea and in polar waters.

Brachiopod

ANCIENT JAWS

Primitive sharks and armored fish lived in the ancient seas 400-340 MYA. The sharks were similar to today's sharks, but the armored fish died out, making way for modern bony fish, such as barracuda.

Today's mako sharks are similar to their prehistoric ancestors.

Cephalapsis was one of the first recognizable fish to appear, about 400 MYA. It had a round, sucking mouth with no movable jaw. A bony, crescent-shaped head shield protected its front end. It was only about 4 inches (10 centimeters) long.

Dinichthys, meaning "terrible fish," was the monster of the seas 400 MYA. A giant predatory fish, 20 feet (6 meters) long, it had a mouth like a shark and large crushing and cutting teeth. Its head end was covered with armor.

Dinichthys

Scientists thought the coelacanth was extinct, until one was caught in the Indian Ocean in 1938. It is a primitive fish, similar to those that gave rise to amphibians 350 MYA. It survives today in the deep sea near the Comoro Islands, Madagascar, South Africa, and the Philippines. Today's small populations are in danger of being overfished.

Coelacanth

Awesome Facts

Megalodon fed on whales and dolphins in coastal waters. Its teeth marks can be found on fossil bones of small whales that are now extinct.

Jamoytius

X

Jamoytius was a jawless fish that lived in freshwater lakes 400 MYA. Coccoteus was an armored fish with a shield covered in bony pimples. Its skull hinged upward like a car hood.

X

Coccoteus

Q: Who had the biggest teeth?

A: The shark megalodon, which was a relative of the modern great white shark. Its body was over 40 feet (12 meters) long and its razor-sharp teeth (right) were 7 inches (18 centimeters) long. It reached its greatest size 12 MYA, and died out about 1.5 MYA. It probably outgrew its food supply.

FEARSOME REPTILES

Long before dinosaurs appeared, giant reptiles roamed the Earth. They were called the mammal-like reptiles, because they looked like modern mammals.

The tuatara lives today in New Zealand, but it has ancient ancestors. It is a living fossil—a leftover from 200 MYA. Tuataras grow slowly: they take 20 years to reach sexual maturity (when they can reproduce). This contributes to the tuatara being an endangered species.

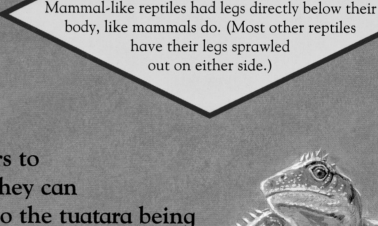

Awesome Facts
Mammal-like reptiles had legs directly below their body, like mammals do. (Most other reptiles have their legs sprawled out on either side.)

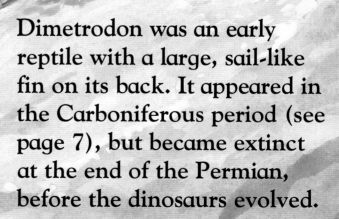

Dimetrodon

Dimetrodon was an early reptile with a large, sail-like fin on its back. It appeared in the Carboniferous period (see page 7), but became extinct at the end of the Permian, before the dinosaurs evolved.

Lystrosaurus was a reptile that looked like the modern hippopotamus. It had wide feet for walking on boggy ground, and eyes and ears on top of its head, suggesting that it spent much time in the water. Its teeth were reduced to tusks, which it probably used to dig up plant roots.

Tuatara

Gorgonopsids were the largest and most ferocious predators on Earth 250 MYA. They were reptiles, but they looked like saber-toothed cats with their large, stabbing canine teeth.

WHEN GIANTS RULED THE WORLD

The dinosaurs and their giant reptile relatives in the sea and air were the dominant animals on Earth 230-65 MYA. A global catastrophe 65 MYA saw them all disappear in an evolutionary blink of an eye.

Tylosaurus

Archelon

Dolphin-like ichthyosaurs, long-necked plesiosaurs, and short-necked mosasaurs terrorized the seas. They were all giants. Archelon, the largest known sea turtle, was over 13 feet (4 meters) across.

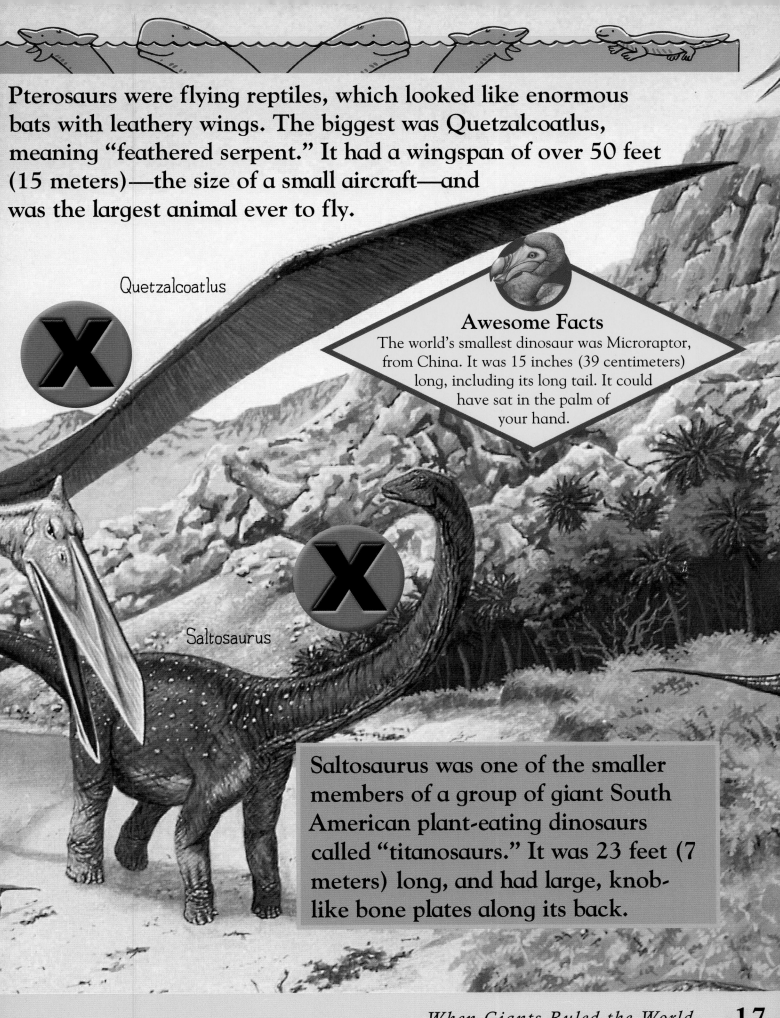

Pterosaurs were flying reptiles, which looked like enormous bats with leathery wings. The biggest was Quetzalcoatlus, meaning "feathered serpent." It had a wingspan of over 50 feet (15 meters)—the size of a small aircraft—and was the largest animal ever to fly.

Quetzalcoatlus

Awesome Facts
The world's smallest dinosaur was Microraptor, from China. It was 15 inches (39 centimeters) long, including its long tail. It could have sat in the palm of your hand.

Saltosaurus

Saltosaurus was one of the smaller members of a group of giant South American plant-eating dinosaurs called "titanosaurs." It was 23 feet (7 meters) long, and had large, knob-like bone plates along its back.

MASS EXTINCTIONS

Six times in the past, huge numbers of living things have been wiped out in catastrophic mass extinctions. There have also been smaller extinction events. The exact causes are unknown, but may have included meteorites hitting Earth from space, volcanic eruptions, and changes in climate and sea level.

Awesome Facts
Scientists are predicting that during the 21st century, there will be another mass extinction of plants and animals on Earth. This time, the culprit will be humans.

Q: Why did mammals survive when the dinosaurs died out?

A: At the time of the dinosaurs, the mammals were very small and could hide away. They had fur and could regulate their body temperature. This helped them to adapt to any changes taking place on Earth. When dinosaurs disappeared, mammals began to fill the niches that dinosaurs had left vacant.

End of the Cambrian (510 MYA)
Sea level changes meant that many species of brachiopods and trilobites found that their former habitats had disappeared. Unable to adapt, they, too, disappeared.

Late Ordovician (400 MYA)
Ice sheets covered the world. Much of the sea froze, and many animals that lived there—echinoderms, ammonites, and more species of trilobites—were left homeless and died.

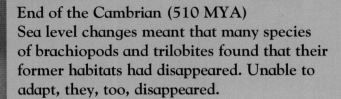

Late Devonian (365 MYA)
A series of small extinctions over a three-million-year period saw 70 percent of warm-water marine species vanish, including early fish and more brachiopods and ammonites.

End of the Permian (250 MYA)
Following 100 million years of stability, life on Earth was hit by the biggest known mass extinction event. Sea level changes, volcanic eruptions, and climate change caused 96 percent of marine species and 75 percent of land vertebrate families (animals with backbones) to become extinct.

Late Triassic (208 MYA)
A relatively modest extinction, when 25 percent of animal families disappeared due to climate change, including increased rainfall.

End of the Cretaceous (65 MYA)
It is thought that a giant meteorite strike and volcanic explosions caused natural environmental pollutions on a huge scale, which caused the extinction of all the dinosaurs, pterosaurs, marine reptiles, and ammonites.

FANTASTIC TITANS

About 38-25 MYA, mammals grew to gigantic sizes, much like the dinosaurs had done. Some species developed bizarre trucks, horns, and tusks. These giants were plant eaters, and ate the leaves of bushes and trees rather than grass. Like the dinosaurs, they also became extinct.

Brontotherium

Brontotherium, or "thunder beast," was one of a group of giant rhinoceros-like animals called "titanotheres." It had strange, forked horns set beside each other on its snout. As the climate became drier, there were fewer bushes and more grass. Brontotherium failed to change its diet and became extinct.

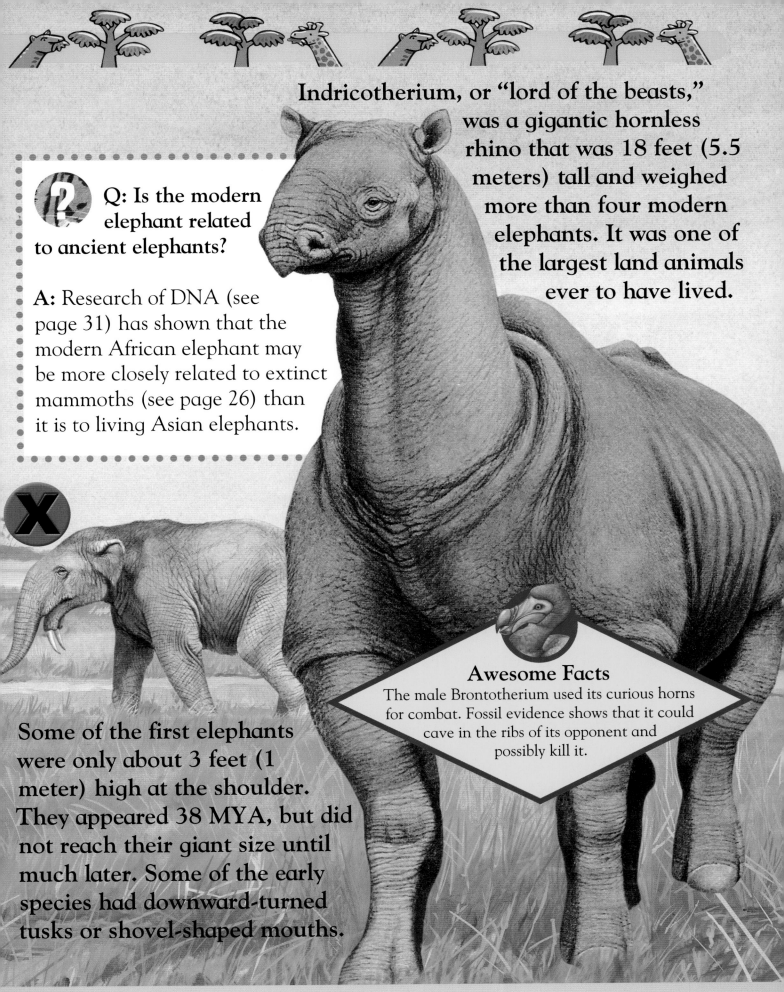

Indricotherium, or "lord of the beasts," was a gigantic hornless rhino that was 18 feet (5.5 meters) tall and weighed more than four modern elephants. It was one of the largest land animals ever to have lived.

Q: Is the modern elephant related to ancient elephants?

A: Research of DNA (see page 31) has shown that the modern African elephant may be more closely related to extinct mammoths (see page 26) than it is to living Asian elephants.

Some of the first elephants were only about 3 feet (1 meter) high at the shoulder. They appeared 38 MYA, but did not reach their giant size until much later. Some of the early species had downward-turned tusks or shovel-shaped mouths.

Awesome Facts
The male Brontotherium used its curious horns for combat. Fossil evidence shows that it could cave in the ribs of its opponent and possibly kill it.

ANCIENT MONSTERS

Many animal groups of the past had their giants. Huge lizards lived in the recent past. Enormous vultures called "teratorns" lived 5 MYA. With a wingspan of 25 feet (7.5 meters), they were the world's largest flying birds. There were also giant penguins as tall as humans.

Zoom in on…

Terror Bird

The "terror bird" Diatryma lived up to its name. It was 10 feet (3 meters) tall and had a huge bill that ripped the flesh off its prey. It was flightless, and lived in what is now South America. It chased and ate primitive horses, which were much smaller than horses are today.

Diatryma was a top predator 50 MYA.

Komodo dragon

The Komodo dragon is a leftover from a bygone age and a living relative of Megalania. It grows to 10 feet (3 meters) long, and lives today on Komodo island, in Indonesia, and neighboring islands. It once feasted on miniature island elephants, but these are now extinct.

Megalania was Australia's giant monitor lizard and the largest land lizard that ever existed. A fully grown adult was about 23 feet (7 meters) long. It fed on the giant ancestors of today's kangaroos and wombats. It lived until 25,000 years ago, and probably confronted Australia's first human settlers.

Megalania

Q: Why do animals grow so big?

A: Animals tend to evolve into giants when conditions on the planet are right. There must be many millions of years without climate change or global catastrophe. These are times when food is abundant. Throughout prehistory, all animal groups have tended toward gigantism at one time or another.

BIG TEETH

During the past 20 million years, catlike creatures with huge canine teeth have appeared several times, in different animal families. This is known as "convergent evolution." There were true saber-toothed cats, saber-toothed ancestors or mongooses, and civet, saber-toothed hyenas, and marsupial sabertooths.

 Q: Why did sabertooths have such big teeth and why did they die out?

A: The giant canine teeth were used to deliver a fatal, slashing wound to the belly or throat of its prey. The sabertooth then waited for its prey to die. The largest known canines were 9 inches (23 centimeters) long. Sabertooths disappeared about 10,000 years ago, when giant plant eaters became extinct and there was competition from smaller, more adaptable predators.

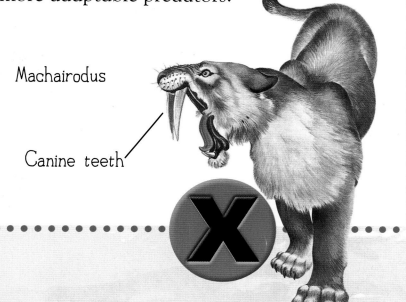

Machairodus

Canine teeth

The North American plains were the hunting ground of the powerful short-faced bear. With long legs like a cheetah, it chased down its prey, which included early horses.

The dire wolf was similar in shape to modern wolves but more robust (stronger). It had shorter, sturdier legs and a larger and broader head. It probably scavenged on the bodies of giant plant eaters.

Thylacasmilus was a marsupial sabertooth about the size of a small tiger. Borhyaena was a marsupial scavenger—it ate meat killed by other animals. They both lived in South America from 10 to 5 MYA.

Borhyaena

Thylacasmilus

MAMMOTHS AND OTHER GIANTS

Mammoths appeared about 20 MYA. They arose in Africa, but moved to all parts of the world, including the Arctic. Most species became extinct about 10,000 years ago. They were not all giants. A species of pygmy woolly mammoth survived until 4,000 years ago.

The woolly rhinoceros lived beside mammoth herds on the Arctic plains, but died out 20,000 years ago.

 Q: Did humans kill off the giant mammals?

A: No one knows for sure. One theory suggests that early people hunted them to extinction. Another proposes that climate change led to their end. A third view holds that people introduced diseases that caused widespread sickness and death among mammals.

Mammoth

The imperial mammoth was the world's largest elephant-like mammal. It stood 14 feet (4.3 meters) at the shoulder. It is now extinct, but it is thought that DNA extracted from frozen carcasses found in Siberia could be transferred into elephant egg cells and implanted in a female elephant. In this way, the mammoth could be reborn.

Megatherium was a giant ground sloth that stood 20 feet (6 meters) on its back legs. It shared the South American continent with early humans, who are thought to have contributed to its extinction 10,000 years ago.

PRIMITIVE PEOPLE

Humans are recent arrivals on the planet, but in the short time we have been around, we have had a devastating effect. Humans were the first creatures to significantly change the environment—and not always for the better.

Homo erectus

Homo habilis

The first humanlike creatures appeared about 3 MYA. They were the ape-men, called "Australopithecus." There was a lightweight form that looked like a chimpanzee, and a more robust form like a gorilla. Next came Homo habilis (handyman), who stood upright and used tools. Then came Homo erectus (upright man), who used sophisticated tools and fire.

Australopithecus

Awesome Facts

Modern humans are more closely related to chimpanzees than chimpanzees are to gorillas.

Before modern humans appeared, there was Homo neanderthalensis (Neanderthal man), who was not as primitive as is sometimes made out. The stocky Neanderthals appeared about 230,000 years ago, and were well adapted to living in cold conditions. They buried their dead and looked after their sick. By 30,000 years ago they had died out, to be replaced by modern humans—Homo sapiens.

Homo neanderthalensis

 Q: Who killed the Neanderthals?

A: Their last stand was in southwest Spain. It is thought that they were forced out of Europe by the changing climate, which had been going in and out of ice ages, or by the advance of sophisticated modern humans who drove them to extinction.

Homo sapiens

BACK FROM THE DEAD

Can ancient animals be brought back to life? It was suggested in the book and film *Jurassic Park* that the blood from blood-sucking insects trapped in amber might be used to extract dinosaur DNA. It is fiction, but a plan to breed a mammoth using DNA extracted from frozen tissues in Siberia could become reality one day.

Q: Who decides when an animal is extinct?

A: The IUCN (International Union for the Conservation of Nature and Natural Resources) coordinates research and assesses the status of surviving species of plants and animals. If a species has not been recorded for over 50 years, it is considered extinct. The hunting and selling of wild animals is monitored by CITES (Convention on Internationals Trade in Endangered Species of Wild Fauna and Flora).

Bulmer's fruit bat was first described from 12,000-year-old fossils found on Papua, New Guinea. It was not until 1975 that the first living bat was found on another part of the island. But as soon as it was discovered, its numbers were reduced by hunters. By 1980, it was feared extinct, but in 1993, a small population of 160 bats was rediscovered.

GLOSSARY

Amphibian
A backboned animal that lives both in water and on land.

Ancestor
A historical forerunner of an animal group.

Canine teeth
The pair of fang-like teeth prominent in some mammals.

Dinosaur
One of many ancient land reptiles that lived from 230 to 65 million years ago.

DNA
Stands for "Deoxyribonucleic acid," a chemical inside every plant and animal cell. DNA carries the information that controls the development of the body for each species.

Endangered
Describes an animal in danger of extinction whose survival is in doubt if the factors causing its decline continue.

Environment
The complete range of conditions in which a plant or animal lives.

Evolution
The process by which all plants and animals appeared, how they developed over time, and how they are still changing gradually today.

Extinct
Describes a species that has not been seen in the wild for over 50 years.

Fossil
The remains of any ancient plant or animal, usually preserved in rock.

Gills
Organs that let underwater animals breathe.

Habitat
The place where an animal lives, usually characterized by the plants that grow there.

Mammal
A backboned animal with hair, such as a cat or a human, which feeds its young on milk.

Marsupial
A mammal that has a pouch in which it keeps its underdeveloped young.

Meteorite
A solid body that has fallen to Earth from space.

Niche
The precise place an animal occupies in a community of plants and animals.

Pollution
Things that can damage the environment, including waste, chemicals, and noise.

Predator
An animal that hunts and eats other animals.

Reptile
A backboned animal with scales that lays eggs, such as a dinosaur or a crocodile.

Species
Animals that resemble one another closely and are able to breed together.

Tusk
An enlarged tooth that projects from the mouth.

INDEX